Deep Shallows

OrangeBooks Publication

Smriti Nagar, Bhilai, Chhattisgarh - 490020

Website: **www.orangebooks.in**

First Edition, 2021
ISBN: 978-93-90837-07-6

DEEP SHALLOWS

MAHIKA BANSAL

OrangeBooks Publication

www.orangebooks.in

"To The Voice
Of Unheard"

Know The Author

Mahika Bansal (pen-name Mahik's), a mere 16 years Indian draws her passion for poetry since the age of 10 and has matured while penning poems for her loving parents on their special occasions. Her first poem was in Hindi and thereafter, she has never looked back. The hobby is now maturing and shaping into a professional mould. The diversity she experiences while discovering different facets of life and observing the stimuli around her, inspires her willingness to pen it down.

Blogging since 12, she has been featured in various sites and magazines including THE BURGUNDY ZINE (is also an active team member there). She is a visiting poet for the US-based ZOETRY and her contribution is showcased in the "MAGPIES: A ZOEM ANTHOLOGY" book as well. Her poem - "BATTLE WARRIORS: THE SOLDIERS" was printed by the renowned Indian newspaper - THE TIMES OF INDIA (TIMES PLUS edition, 19 January 2020 issue). Her podcast episode with "CAN YOU TELL ME A STORY?" was quite an insightful. Her debut with the music single VIBES AT SIXTEEN (written by Mahik's) has got her accolades.

These are just some recent feathers in her cap. The achievements are only growing with the days.

Hailing from Moradabad, Uttar Pradesh, India, she aims at inking words while trying to be the voice of the unheard. Apart from "being in Mahik's mode," she can be found listening to music, vibing with friends, cuddling with the family or just being a confused teen, oops! She loves interacting with new people via twitter/mail. She prefers comprehensive chats over a cuppa with cookies.

For the perfect description of the beliefs and theories she holds, her interview with SUMMATION 52 (https://www.summation52.com/post/featured-artist-mahika-bansal) can be tuned into.

Page credits-

Col Sanjay Chawla (Retd), SM

All About
Deep Shallows

Instead of the infinite wordy combinations to crown this book, why did the author pick these two words- DEEP SHALLOWS specifically? The writer has set her heart on diving into the various extensive intellects and too, revealing the superficial, yet overlooked shallow themes. Life is very mere, but mortals have termed it as intricate. We often leave some simple cues of the profound secrets. Those are again the deep shallows.

As you read further, you'll walk into the world of words that are ultimately relatable to all of us.

Precious reader, you are stepping in, to travel on an unexpected journey. You're a dreamer, *Mahik's* is a poet. Both are the keys to one another's locks! Your insightful views inspire the poet to unlock more rhythmic mysteries! Likewise, the inked pages of this book are your tickets to unhitch the reality by sailing into a fantasy! Did this oxymoron amaze you? Well, you're about to discover more about the DEEP SHALLOWS!

Acknowledgements

A token of appreciation to all those who stood by me and believed in my journey as a young poetess.

Earnestly, my parents are the solid base of who I am today. I found them backing me when I didn't even know how to talk. They held my hand in every step I ever took. Sacrifices, affection, tears, and smiles,… I can never know or realize what it took for them to be so crystal pure and idealistic! Apologies for anytime that I hurt them.

My friends, my extended family, and my loved ones! What can I even say? Their support means the world to me. They make my life magical.

Sincere gratitude to Col Sanjay Chawla (retd) for beautifying my book blurb and "know the author" page. His editing has added more importance to my book. I regard the aid and the time spent.

Special acknowledgment to Rainbow Creative Vision Pvt. Ltd. (Mr. Ankit Bansal) for helping me bring this book to life! Book designing is a significant process in book publishing and I am glad to have the provided help.

And loads of love to all my readers! My blog and my book were all possible because of them. I thank each one from the bottom of my heart. Thank you for picking my book and investing the precious time reading the work.

In my life, everything I have observed, felt and everyone I have ever met is a part of what I do and who I am. I always say that everything around me inspires me. So, thanks a million for being an encouragement and a stimulus. I wish to continue this journey lifelong. My heart is full of excitement for whatever the future
holds and I hope that you are ready too :)

Contents

Twilight

She's the sunrise,
refreshing and flashy.
Dancing and rolling
shades of skies,
and clouds,
patchy.

He's the dusk.
Sparkle of the
magical eventide
with the scent of musk
matching the scene,
a deep, breezy ride.

One has new hopes,
the other soul is wild.
Yet both are entangled
together,
serene in dive and rise.

She jumps off the start,
travels like no one can.
She creates her own art,
the world fails to understand.

He is calm. He is shy.
He vanishes away.
The pollen too, flies.
His home? A secret place.
Sophistication resides.

When he sees her,
from miles apart,
the sky, a love-struck fond.
Birds fly like a heart,
betoken the eternal bond.

Fellowship is puzzled…
Is he so surreal
or is she so bright?
But up in the air,
the sky reveals
Heaven lies
in the twilight!

My Life Is Just

My life is just like a pen and page
where I write my world in words.
God gifted me a book to ink
and save it from the dirt.

My life is just like a coffee mug
which I fill with soothing love.
It may not be of your flavor
but I like it, I make it work.

My life is just like how a movie runs
where God knows what happens next.
But I don't know the twist and turns,
I always live in suspense.

My life is just like a story tale
where the hero is me.
In the first half, I tend to fail,
But in end runs away my enemy.

Oh, my life is such a rainbow,
several colors to show.
Not green or grey, may I just say
I got a perfect blend; I know!

Mahika Bansal

The Humsum Days

Wrinkles on the skin with a grave grey beard,
carrying a plump lens in hand and memory smeared.

Teeth fallen out, ears asleep,
unaware of my smile or my weep.

More time to pass, less to live.
I blabber my stories in a not-so peachy plink.

With no audience afar, as I sit in lone
on my rocking chair, I swing and sometimes groan.

I oft think 'bout my life past long.
All the memories I can remember prolong.

I can't recall my pills or your name,
but I can still hark back to my kid's nonage.

I can't spot my coffee mug or my house keys,
yet I am sure about all the clips my eyes did see.

I have reminiscences of all these years.
I oft' times forget, but out of the blue they reappear.

This time's operations, I may not know,
but I have seen the earth change and plants grow.

I have seen success, struggles and fails,
I have had a beloved family, which now half prevails.

I'm being forgotten now, oh lord!
I can't work anymore, so I'm being ignored.

I'm a burden for all, since I can't move.
My knees are far fragile to reprove.

It's almost time to leave everything behind
and heavenly stairs when I climb.

But before that, I just want that last hug,
for I'll always love this amazing world.

Don't shred my chattel so promptly, please!
Let me relive in your memoir dreams.

Mahika Bansal

The Laughing Jaws!

I hear some laughing jaws
with their nasty heads along.
They laugh at everything,
whether right or wrong.

Their creepy weird eyes,
their stupid giggling smiles.
About them, it says all.
I call 'em the laughing jaws.

With a motive to demotivate,
they relish the spreading hate.
But some of us just don't care,
and their plan disastrously fails.

Omnipresent everywhere,
gleeful chuckles on our flaws.
How we deal with them is our call
'cause they are the laughing jaws.

Pour Out

Always thought that poetry means to
flow as it goes, a rhythmic song.
Had to rhyme, to be raw, and
catch the tune along, but
then I wrote this verse
and I perceived,
poetry
is 'bout
thoughts.

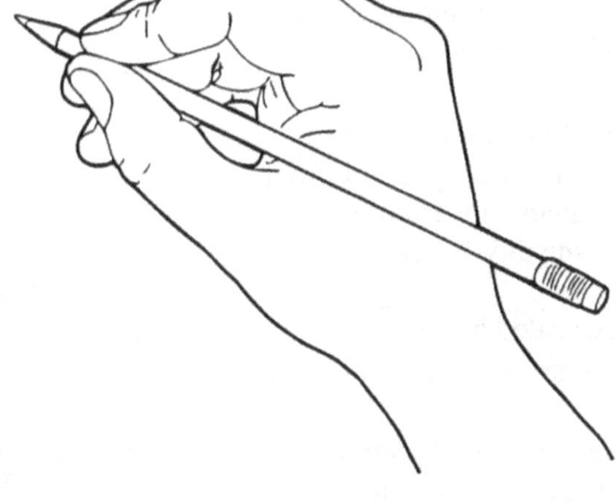

**This poem is a NONET- A poem with 9 lines and no rhyme. Syllable count goes as such- foremost line contains 9 syllables, second line with 8, third line with 7 syllables... and it goes on in a manner that the finishing line is left with 1 syllable count.*

Red

She was a garden of roses,
and you grew in them the needles.
She was a red carpet of petals.
Now there's bleeding blood, no creedal.

The red paint drew a portrait,
journey of being shredded into loom
which portrayed.

You left your brush there
and ran away from the frame.
She knew it was unfair
but she didn't share
her pain.
She sealed her lips,
watched you taking no blame.

She understood your game!
but she felt it was accurate
to let you go.
Or else you might hurt her again.
Again… someday.

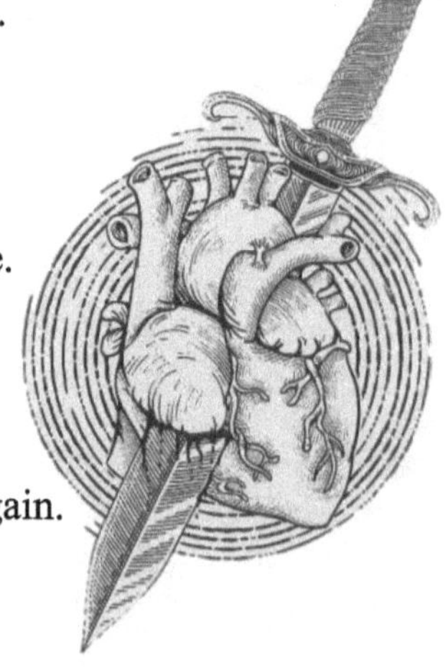

Glitters In The Sky

Shadow of the moon
seems as crystals of the sky,
falling into the clear sea
catching all of my sight.

Starting with glimmering stars,
I could "sea" the glittering waves
ending with flashes at the shore.
Wind makes the trees wave.

I think that patchy beam does lie.
It sleeps or has the open eyes.
It makes me unsure but I would say,
no one beats that magical smile.

The smile of moon has different sides.
I see the half and full sometimes.
The sand at shore is loft to step.
Night makes one get in its shell.

But the crazy me denies
to sleep.
I wake all night,
and enjoy the scene.

Getting some chills,
I chill with me,
Feeling relaxed and calm
and carefree!

Mahika Bansal

Hardship Over Heart-Ship

Crumbled, broken, dull, and lost,
the dark way through
I gnaw. I moan. I craw. I walk.
The path is scary gloom.
Dumb, clueless, strange wanders.
Shivers sharp as swords appear.
My dead-head ponders,
"what if…" I fear.

The wind shovels the blue on me.
I stand still, alas!
My owl eyes refuse to see
any hopes for the time to pass.
I become a clock with no hands-
Inutile, inept, non-existent.

The only tie holding the hand
to keep my soul persistent,
is a couplet, lie or true,
I have no clue-
" Dead or alive, I shall reach the place!
I'm half dead already, hard to trace! "

Live Lyrically

Life plays us like melodic keys,
moody and musical, as it feels.
I'm the song, also the rest
is the rhythm along, I weave my nest.
Seldom I get lost in notes,
that's when I let my soul flow.
Strings and keys get hit hardcore,
but that lets out the best score.
The music we create lifelong
is what's played as a diary song,
when the melody inside us stops the pen,
and we overcome the aroma, amen!

Mahika Bansal

Hopes Of A Huckster...

I am a peddler; I peddle around.
As a hawker, you say.
I am a local, sell for a pound,
earn in pennies per day.

I am a soul who can be found
on every street, I suppose.
To call you mate, I sing aloud.
And you'll never find me close.

Seasons arrive and stay, then leave.
I observe all at a verge.
Sales undone bring huge tension, I grieve,
but then a new day, and hopes emerge.

I am a wanderer in need of cash.
To towns and towns, I go.
Enough food I find in trash,
to feed me and my household.

I desire to hold and build someday
some assets of my own.
But I am a human, though a stray,
so presently, I hope you soften your tone :)

Dejected Dawn...
Dreamy Dusk

Not all words deserve to be heard,
not all to be screamed.
Not all fears need to be conquered,
not everyone lives their dreams.
Every chance is worth
but it doesn't always lead us well.
Encashing the time
is still better than hell.

You'll someday get ditched.
Other time, praised.
Some sunshine will be a delight,
some breaths will bring a craze.

Days do rock
but clocks, too, cling.
Dazzling dolphins or cawing crows,
whatever it brings!
But hidden deep inside,
a little music is in all souls.
Life's like that, so just smile
as big as it can grow!

Mahika Bansal

The Flashy Screens, Today's Enemy

At a party or in school,
you're too busy being cool.
The likes and hashtags,
the fake "you" on snapchat.
Eyes down and neck bend
on flashy screens, that's the trend.

Never wish to meet in real,
texting is meant to be ideal.
Don't speak a word to one near
but your posts show as you're chilling up here.

Don't know what's the pun in pics,
why to hide your face in all the clicks.
The swag is being rude in selfie.
Want to look mad? Kay, then be.

Someday we used to play in air,
now the virtual games are all you care.
We used to laugh at jokes or weep in pain.
Now you send an emoji, no emotions to name.

You ain't humane, no respect or gratitude.
You ain't have a thing but just attitude.
So what if we weren't so smart with gadgets growing
up?
We still live in the real, not in the man-made world.

Oh, what screens have done to us!
'Twas there to connect people. Plus,
gather knowledge and explore it to sky.
Now look at you, what happened and why?!

The life today is all fake.
You know nothing but a story to update.

Mahika Bansal

Life

I am blind, though see the world.
With closed eyes, I observe.
I am dumb, yet not shut.
In the silence, my thoughts are heard.
I am deaf, still listen to talks.
It's not easy to know me folks.

I am Life!

Battle Warriors: The Soldiers

I wish I was a superhero,
dapper in olive.
Always serve my nation first,
before I wish to live.

The superhero of my dream
wears a cape of blessing,
with a missile as a weapon.
That's so impressing!

Point of the sharp sword
splits the light of sunshine,
when the hero wins the war,
and thanks the power divine.

I wish I could have the same
as my symbol sign.
I wish I could imbibe the pain
and make it carpe diem!

I wish I was one soldier
with courage as my power.
With responsibility on my shoulder,
just like they are.
Their strength is their bravery.
They excel in every field.
Oh! That's who I want to be,
who's there when we need!

Mahika Bansal

Wish I could protect my world
from pain and decease,
like a superhero, not in words.
Actions make them freeze.

I will never, ever avert
when my people are in danger.
Instead, I'll be alert
from the witty, wicked stranger.

I'll serve my nation
till my last breath.
Special would be this relation,
You can't guess its depth.

Wrapped in the national flag, oh wow!
On my martyrdom.
That's all I want to be paid,
for my wisdom.

Fiction has many
but the country has one,
that's a princely patriot,
a mother's true son.

* Printed by the renowned Indian newspaper -
THE TIMES OF INDIA (TIMES PLUS edition, 19 January 2020 issue)

Mahika Bansal

Stage Spotlight, Delight Or Plight?

A deep cry within my heart.
My feet stood still before could I start.
A scary thought in my mind
that left me numb, blank, and blind.
A miserable noise heard my ears,
I shut 'em down and shed in tears.

A shock was there in my hair.
The feeling was weird, solemn, and rare.
My tongue was cut and heart gloom.
I jerked my hand and left the room.

My name in headlines was all I wished before.
Well, I still got my treat, but 'twas sore.
That day set an insane score.
Thy touchdown, but mine, a slip on the floor.

Those talks for me
still pinch my soul.
I hear them to date
and it breaks me whole.

"Where I was," "when was it,"
don't ask, it's just that I quit.
'Cause if I share the full tale with you,
all we'll hear is "boooooooo...."

For I let ye know, I managed that time, but again, can't I.
I won't get up to that stage for those stupid smiles.
Or I'll break anew for the same thing,
alike that night, when I stopped to sing.

Mahika Bansal

The Silent Sea

One day, I came across a sea.
Refreshing tides was the sight I could see.
Chattering leaves in the cold breeze.
I wish the moment I could seize.

I quietly sat down on the sand.
It felt like a serene of the pleasant land.
I thought it was the best place
for our strained mind to find a calm space.
If one is alone or in pain,
the entire smile the soul can gain.

Glitch

I open my mouth to hear
that I have a disgusting tongue.
People burst their tears
to say that I'm spoiled young.

If I shut my mouth,
World labels me ignorant.
If my soul cries in public,
I'm belligerent.

People shed their loans on me
how they have managed my survival.
As a curse I feel,
because they think I don't care either.

I still don't get in my head,
why people think I don't give a damn.
Like I'm an evil brat,
but in reality, I care, and it cramps.

Mahika Bansal

I don't think I can change 'em,
I don't know what to change in me.
Should I talk or stay quiet or
Leave it as it is, creepy?

I tried to talk it out
but the world labeled me crazy.
I even locked my life and shout.
All I got was a depressed me.

So I wrote it down
to take my frustration somewhere
'cause I wanted to wipeout
the bleeding tears.

The Life of Teens

Ripped jeans, touch screens.
The whole life of teens
revolves around the fashion about,
starts and even ends with these.

These teens, these tweens,
the junk food extreme.
Some like to live on diet meals,
while some hate the greens.

It looks so cool,
the amazingly perfect.
But it's not that easy,
there're some defects.

It's an age
of finding the true you.
The one who's here,
and in future too.

They're not kids,
to play with sand.
But still not mature and big,
alone to stand.

It's typical
when they have to choose
the way to go,

the step of shoes,
their nature to live through-
ego or smile,
floor to the roof,
the correct path of life.

The teens, the tweens,
need your support.
They might get upset,
'cause they don't know-

You are their guide
for the entire life.
The one whose advice
is best and precise.

They are not aware
that you are there
as their best dude,
So special, so true.

Beyond

I,
standing
miles apart
can hear your heart,
whimsical calm laugh
or chaotic crying cold.
I wish that I could come home.
But has one ever returned back?
Shall the mortal live once, die one day,
relive life in thy heart again, they say.

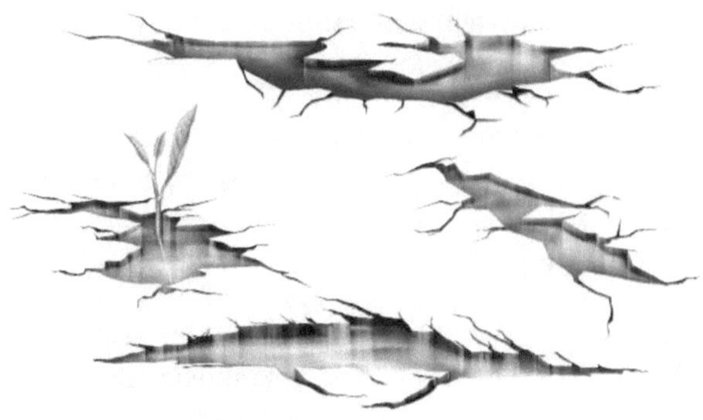

**ETHEREE form of poetry- A typical poem of this kind consists of 10
unrhymed lines with an ascending syllable count with each line. This etheree
has a little twist! This poem <u>rhymes</u> but has 10 line with the necessary syllable
counting of an etheree.*

Mahika Bansal

Musical Me

The rap notes when hit my head,
I nod and dance and spring my neck.
When rhythms so smooth soothe my ears,
I bring back the memories back in years.
When I freak out with my heavy brain,
I play my music to kill the pain.
Pals when come to rock my day,
I turn on speakers and sounds I make.

When I need and what I want,
my songs know me, strong is our bond.
I shed my tears or take over fears,
I rock my mood or dreams come near.

The language of music knows me well,
when world can't feel me, music can.
It speaks when all silent themselves.
When it comes to music,
I'm speechless.

Hi To Green, Goodbye To Grey

There was a forest long ago,
no roads for to and fro.
Through the woods
we used to go.
Now this place
is full of roads.

There used to be,
long dense trees,
and fresh air
all around.
Now there are
tall buildings.
Forests are cut down.

Sweet chirps
in the morning,
some terrifying
sounds at night.
The morning breeze
was so refreshing,
so was sunset's sight.

Where we should feel the nature,
now we hesitate to go out.
God is its maker,
save it somehow.

Now all we have is polluted air,
chemicals and plastics, oh no!
Now we have to clean this world,
some seeds we have to sow.

This place we have to save.
Make sure this land is safe.
Now it's our responsibility,
to break this nasty cave.

Unwinding

Hot cocoa to soothe the soul,
a cozy blankey for cold feet.
Stressed and tired, cushions to console,
headsets to feel the moody beat.

Closed eyelids, show a miraculous world
where the body meets spirit.
Alive, yet see a paradise pearl,
a galaxy unvisited.

Wearing a beanie,
lay on the bean bag,
dodge the mean-ie,
No chaos to drag.

Dim lights to bring in peace,
detached from the mankind.
If someone takes a leave,
hope people wouldn't mind.

Even if they do,
they simply don't exist
in your heaven, somewhat true,
tells what life should consist.

Wretched Yet No Regret

A lonesome horror to live in,
"crap" soup to eat,
spook stuff to play with,
and no soul to speak.

Far from town,
not a single bird chirps.
Paths on roads
have cracks and jerks.

Blinks the light,
dooms the sun.
Curse-like plight,
and there's nothing I have done.

No way out,
I'm stuck in such a dream
where fairy tales too
end in screams.

Once, my sorrow
struck my mind
and then I
began to write

a spooky spank-y poem
written in atrocious tears
and as you read the tone,
all seems so queer.

But if it never would've betided,
I won't have this legend
for me to write and you to read,
The dirt of this gem!

Mahika Bansal

Springz Knocking!

Luscious grass so green so fresh.
The bees on blooms of flowery mesh.
Chirps and chicks, all around,
so calm, so cool and chill it sounds.

Kids on swings and birds with wings.
The sunlight strings with a breezy wind.
The blinking glister as some glitter
of light in patches, so little tittle.

Whoosh whoosh whoosh,
that's wind's push.
Chee chee chee,
that voice is so sweet.
All that makes the perfect scene.

Broom Not Bloom

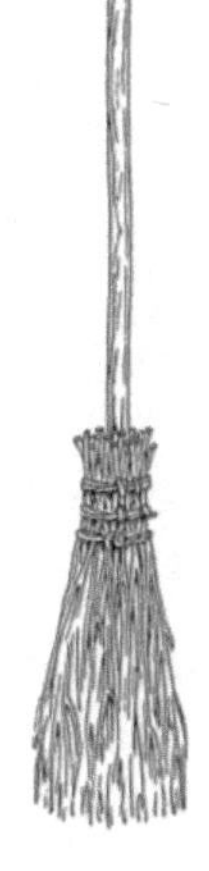

Once came in my way,
a small helpless boy
with a broom in hand,
not a book or toy.

Jeans rugged and old,
his shirt had holes,
was in an uproar,
a one less hope.

Tiny little hands,
dull crying eyes,
screaming yet shut lips,
skin brittle and dry.

Looked up to me
with a tear in his eye.
He kept mum
but I heard his outcry.

I was up in the bus
and in foot he stood,
willing to be like us,
if he could.

I saw him for a while,
then my bus passed by
but he was still in my sight
and it made me realize.

There are many out there,
alike as him.
No one to care,
Living near bins.

I saw many others before,
but never thought this way.
A better life to them,
my only pray.

The following day,
I searched him on street.
For unknown reasons,
I wanted to meet.

I couldn't do much,
I know!
He was just like us,
I wanted to show.

I tried to help all I can
but, my bad!
I never saw him again.

A Lash With A Splash

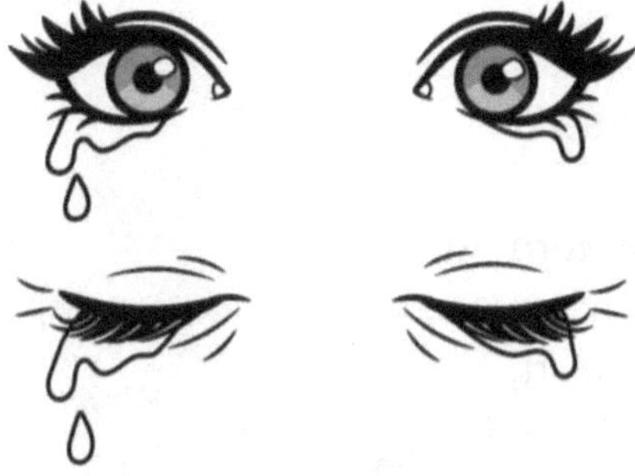

A lash falls out, whenever you cry.
It sheds off from your teary wet eye.
Whenever a lash comes off, don't let it go.
Make a wish, give a blow and let it flow.

A new one will grow back in time
to match your beautiful face and rhyme.
It'll be a start of something new,
as the hair curl back on anew.

And it'll trip over and above,
will return back every time but
the newborn won't come out, it'll refrain,
until your tears come back again.

Mahika Bansal

Trampled Pages, Guilty Rages

That one chapter,
we all have.
Those crumpled pages,
thrown in trash.

The chapter torn off,
crumbled and crushed,
trashed by heart,
memories flushed.

Splashes it gave,
thy wiped it up.
Inked pages of life,
were to be reversed.

Erased couldn't it be,
but withdrawn.
As you pleased,
you moved on.

Rightly done, but yet,
as a daunt it acts.
The dent it left,
they haunt, leaving deep impacts.

Blood on sword
is the color of shame.
Day and night, you implore,
your mind to forget the sins.

The vexation you show
tapping pencils on that book,
wish to burn it with a roar,
the depressing words it took.

You still try to hide,
the frustrating fights in head.
But mind will go wild
if you keep it under the bed.

So advice all the blithe took
is one shall never keep a track.
Mantra to peace is to never memoir a book
'cause life can never get packed.

In a book so thin, or as fat,
a tough hardcover, or a smooth paperback.
So, just flow with the wind
and break the pen, a tested fact!

Mahika Bansal

The Utopian Cologne

Yes, I'm lost,
away from the road
I walk,
where go my toes.

Boots in fist and
hair bounce and swirl.
The grass at verge land,
touch my bare feet, I whirl.

I'm lost in a fantasy,
somewhere unknown.
A wonderland ecstasy,
a utopian cologne.

There, I shoot snaps from eyes
and store 'em in heart.
I go as I smile,
I make my own paths.

Yes, I'm lost
'cause I leave no pixie dust.
I live in my thoughts.
At least calm is that world.

Un-Healed

Unfeared fears oft leave
screeched scars, better boldly show
what stitches can't heal.

**Inked in the form of a Japanese poetry, this verse is a HAIKU. This form is
written in 3 lines with the syllable count of 5-7-5.*

A Truth From My Weeping Eyes!

Life was so much, quaint when you didn't know how to
drive,
had cement in your hands or know how to bribe.
When plastic was unknown and forests were elite,
when I was worshipped with a grace, not trodden under
your feet.

Oh, those days were good,
when the dictionary had no words
like war, hate, hurt, kill, or the ones that destroy me, "the
Earth."
Now my face is turning pale, 'cause my colors- green
and blue
are vanishing away so quick, and it's just because of
you.

You cut my leafy hands and put on them your builds.
You loaded me with tons like you, and others you killed.
Soon you started to hate each other, and called out for
wars,
then technology had to come, just to build firewalls.

You now have bullets in your heart, and greed in mind.
Today there's no place left, where peace I find.
I liked you more when you all were human beings.

You were then humane humans but now, just the dregs
of zombies.

I know you'll hate the bitter truth, but today I say,
you are not the same creature, the masterpiece I made.
You still are my kid though, and I want you to be the
best,
but it hurts me to see you crumbled in all the mess.

I gave you everything I could, but look what you did!
Now everything you do is like an attempt to kill
me, and if I die, you won't survive a day
'cause there's no science of yours,
by which my twin can be made.

A Call For Help...
For We, To Us

I have got so much to speak to you,
problems I face and the fun I do.
But don't know where to start and end.
Whom to meet? Where to wend?

To you I'm a fellow unknown
but still, you hear me, I know.
And I thank you for that you pay attention,
but to change yourself is never your intention.

You know my most poems show today's truth,
the problems and confusions within the youth.
You read my words and think deep,
wish to change a bit but then you sleep.

The next morning you forget me,
my words, my concerns, my poetry.
I know you feel the same what I write
'cause I am one of you and I don't let it be blind.

My words are not new or fiction,
of wrong or right, it's my confession,
Which you all know but don't react.
You should too admit but you step back.

I dare you all to start right this sec,
step ahead and move out from the desk,
bring a change in whatever is flawed,
not for me, but for the lord.

Yeah, poetry is my hobby, my passion and love.
But I don't just write to impress, but above
that I am a dreamy human who dreams of a paradise
world.
So I try to change the globe through touching hearts by
words.

But if you just read, think, forget and move on,
then with generations it'll pass on.
The mistakes will not change, and everyone will suffer.
All will need a revolution but behave like duffers.

They'll yell inside to make things right.
But now and then, no one will spill the guts to fight.
Then one day,
everything will vanish away.

Look at that, if you ignore just a tiny thing,
what can happen, the world can sink.
Forget my poems, read anything that motivates.
But I beg, please don't stay and wait.

Make an effort to make sure
that what you regret should not the kids anymore.
What you suffer, what gives you pain,
Change the whole damn thing!

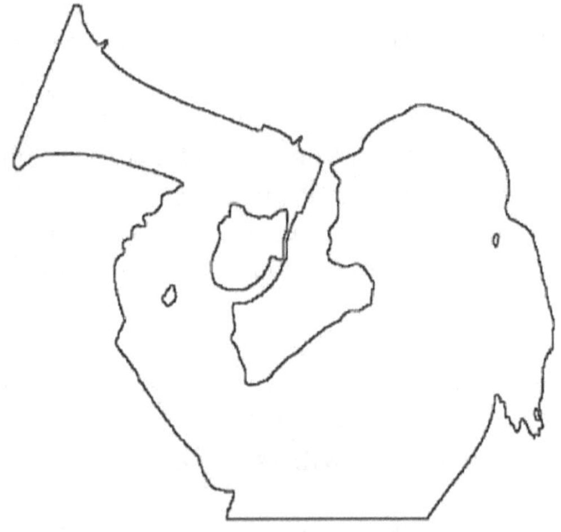

Unseen, Unnoticed, Unfelt

A bracelet once gifted
was charmed, and no one knew.
Adding charms to it, lifted
smiles brand new.

A step once taken
molded a path, and no one was tuned.
Stepping on the past,
contemporary enchanted the fortune.

Air once inhaled
affected, and no one had a clue.
fusing mortal to death, failed
and a longer life, it drew.

Thought once thought
had a reason and no one noticed.
A glimpse was caught,
could unveil secrets, if focused.

A poem once written
had a purpose that most didn't see.
The weaved rhythm had it hidden,
like the roots of a tree.

Mahika Bansal

Cut The Crap!

A little girl with pretty pure eyes,
short curls and innocent cry.
Do you wonder what she wants from life?
I bet, she dreams of a paradise.

She gets told to be big and strong,
to stay jolly and sing a song.
Live carefree 'cause she is the queen,
the princess of everyone's dreams.

But then, she grows up and
how wrong it was, she understands.
A bliss and smile was in her thoughts,
but she didn't know the fights to be fought.

The girl unaware of the silly mindset,
the discrimination, the ridiculous heads,
the misery of every girl in society,
the bad intentions and impiety.

She gets dirt to do and works of low wage.
She is ordered to marry at quite a young age.
She gets denied of works which boys are free for,
her dreams are crushed and what not!

It's pathetic for a little girl to step,
in a world so creepy and full of crap.
Life is pictured as a white precious pearl,
it's for everyone here but a girl.

She is expected to stay inside four walls,
and a fairy this girl is called?!
What kind of a person you expect her to be?
She is just a girl, not to serve to your slavery.

And here it comes, the worst of all,
the crimes done against these pretty dolls.
And still, this is her life, she is blamed for it,
her gender, her freedom, her outfit.

"Cut the crap" is a voice you will hear
if you stop your rubbish talks and feel.
A crying heart is all you'll see,
a livid, ignored, a deep scream.

"Independence" is a thing we girls demand.
A day without hearing- Don't do this or that.
The poor "security" of ours is your fault,
you didn't teach the boys to respect but taunt.

Huh?! You ask me what is wrong with it?
What about our independence and will?
Why live a life according to others?
Why bear everything and not say that it bothers?

Why to move on your say?
I'm not your slave!
Equal in power, we are,
then why are you in heaven and I, in dark?

This is a note to the ones like you,
suggestions are welcome but I won't let you rule.
The society, so conservative and mean,
dare not put your nose in between.

"Don't show us big dreams if you can't
let us decide and do what we want.
The fake fantasy, the one you stream
in our life, crushing our own dreams".

I am bold enough to handle myself.
I don't need you to control my life and compel.
Boundaries and compulsions are not for me.
If I treat you the same, how will you feel?

Nothing much is left to say
'cause you people have empty brains.
Nothing will affect you until I
gather with others and fight.

This poem is a shame for this world,
there shouldn't be a situation to use these words.
Alas! No choice you leave for me
but to fight and cut the C-R-A-P.

Do you wanna know who I am?
I AM EVERY GIRL STANDING ON THIS LAND!

Introspection

I had no version,
just living my heart out.
I was a person,
I didn't ever doubt.

I had no shades,
my aura was pure,
fresh, until you came
and gave wounds to cure.

Injected blisters in my bliss,
my negatives, you did pick.
Made me believe that I don't fit.
I failed to recognize that you're a prick.

I remolded as you
to be accepted
as a member of the crew,
I became deceptive.

The attention of folks
was charming enough.
But I was hidden under a cloak.
The new me, a bluff.

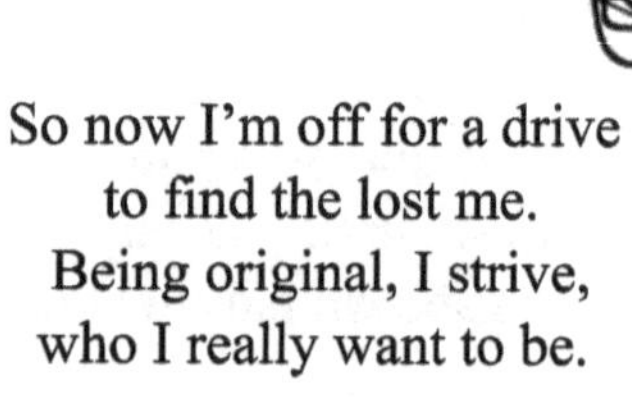

So now I'm off for a drive
to find the lost me.
Being original, I strive,
who I really want to be.

Intimate

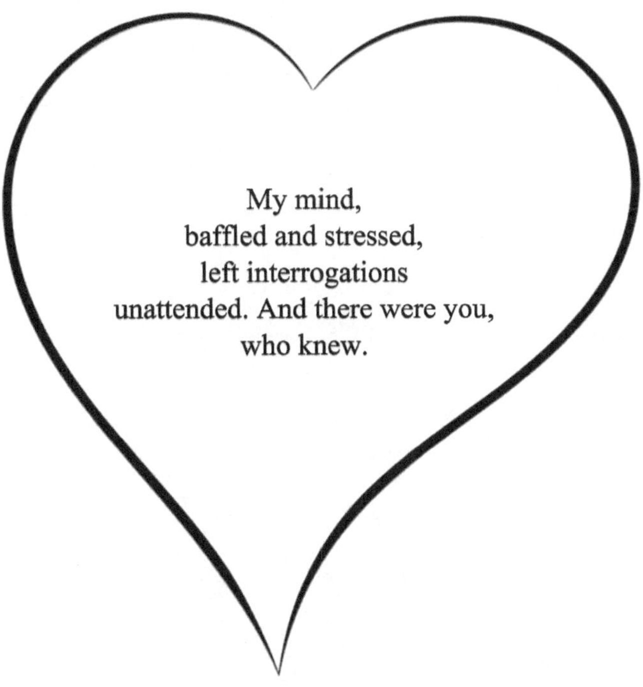

This poem is penned down in the form of CINQUAIN in which, the 1st line contains 2 syllables, 2nd has 4 syllables, 3rd line with 6 syllables, 4th with 8 and the 5th line has 2 syllables.

www.ingramcontent.com/pod-product-compliance
Lightning Source LLC
Chambersburg PA
CBHW051458140726
47987CB00006B/2763